SETTING
YOURSELF UP TO
THRIVE
WITH
DECISIONS

SAMSON UMURHURHU

SETTING YOURSELF UP TO THRIVE WITH DECISIONS

ISBN: 978-978-795-946-6

Published by:
Zayzee Limited
South Pointe Estate, Off Orchid Hotel Road, Lekki, Lagos, Nigeria.
+234 8120259068
zayzeeblog@gmail.com
www.zayzeewrites.com

DEDICATION

To all who want to set themselves up to THRIVE with decisions.

Table of Contents

7·

Acknowledgements

9·

Preface

17·

Chapter One
Relevance Of Decisions
For Thriving

23·

Chapter Two
Thrive-Based And Thrive-
Centred Decisions

43·

Chapter Three
Ingredients For Making
Decisions — With The Potential
To Set You Up To Thrive

55·

Chapter Four
Impacts Of Human Limitations
On Our Decisions

65·

Chapter Five
Conclusion

71·

About The Author

ACKNOWLEDGEMENTS

I woke up one morning with deep realisations and ideas flooding my mind, that people thrive with decisions. I immediately got to work organising these ideas, while reflecting on my own life and those of relevant others. The outcome has become this book. For this, I am grateful for the calling and special favour on my life.

Over the years, I have enjoyed unwavering support from Carol, my dear wife. Her valuable contributions to making decisions have set us up to thrive in our lives and endeavours. I thank her immensely.

To our two children, Aghogho and Ejiro, thank you for your encouragement and insightful input.

Uzezi Adesite, my editor and publisher, thank you for your understanding and guidance to get this book published.

PREFACE

Your decisions are yours. The consequences of your decisions are also yours. Your decisions can empower you and set you up to thrive amid life's challenges, or, entrap you in a situation, pull and bring you down in ruins. When you refuse to make decisions, you have already made a bad decision; a wrong one. Wrong decisions will not help you achieve your best, unless you take a detour to undo those wrong decisions with the right ones, and have a fresh start.

The best policy is to invest in making good or right decisions, capable of advancing you progressively to your envisaged destination. Behind everyone who succeeds and thrives, are decisions taken that set them up.

How often do you ask how well the decisions you want to make or have made are impacting your life? It is not news that we all go through different situations in life. But when faced with different situations, do we make appropriate decisions that give us the power and chance to make a difference in what we are experiencing?

You can become more aware and intentional in positioning your decisions to support and serve you better. You create who you are and become, with your decisions. Your decision, followed by the relevant actions, is your change maker. In your decisions, target as your desired outcome, the most impactful points/ areas of value creation. Your decisions are important; they are a critical factor in determining the quality of your life. They make the intangible tangible. Use your decisions to create the greatest desirable impact and value in the situation you find yourself. Your decision is either your open door or closed door. You hold the key to changing the course of your life, one decision at a time. Your everyday choices and decisions matter.

THRIVE

How do I view the term thrive? Some other words that come to my mind, which reflect what I mean, and want to say or describe are amongst others:

flourish, overcome, do well, blossom, prosper, rise, achieve success, shine, expand, develop, grow, stand out, turn out well, conquer, fly high …. on the foundation of who you are.[1]

When you're *thriving*, you're moving towards your goals and vision, in the midst of and despite your challenging situations and events. In the process, you keep adapting, adjusting, evolving and coming out better equipped to live life, leveraging on your newly acquired experiences and competencies in helping others become better.[2]

---

1 From my book, ***Thriving On Who You Are***
2 Same as above

DECISION

What does the term *decision* mean to me? Some other words that come to my mind, which reflect what I mean, and want to say or describe are amongst others:

choice, position, stand, outcome, result, judgment, resolution, conclusion ... on a specific subject or situation.

A decision is what you come to after you have looked at, evaluated and considered all inputs for options on a subject or situation. This enables you determine the best line of action for your adoption in that particular subject or situation. It is your resolution and conclusion for optimum results.

People and Decisions

We all face challenges and are called to make decisions every day. A vast number of people have great ambitions and dreams of success and thriving. Unfortunately, a peep into some personal situations people are faced with, reveals the reality; lives that are off the course of what they desire.

This happens when people adopt approaches that do not support the delivery of the kind of vision they have for themselves. It also happens when they are incapable of resolving the endless list of battles resulting from wrong decisions and bad choices. Again, correct decisions taken could have been implemented at the wrong times. Also, long-term decisions may have been based on temporary situations, which in some cases, trap people in the wrong places and relationships, thus putting their lives on hold. The divide between that great ambition or dream they had and the reality they live, becomes often traceable to decisions that have left them disempowered, and in which they had compromised their worth, leaving other people to dictate their actions and destinations in life.

Oftentimes, we underestimate the stack-up impacts of the decisions we make. Your decisions can help you or hurt you. With your decisions, you can change things and make better things happen. Certain situations get worse as a cumulative effect of undesirable decisions. You have the power to bring about the change you desire. You can also determine when your change process begins. You can set yourself up to thrive.

Make up your mind and decide. Focus on decisions that can set you up to thrive. Staying put, waiting or doing nothing, is a bad decision. It makes situations worse and more difficult.

Lose no more time. You can do something. You can reverse the trend, and set yourself to go better and higher. The power to do this lies in your decisions and willingness to execute your actions. Making wise and sound decisions is vital for you to succeed and thrive.

Do you know certain people who appear to know exactly what to do in any given situation? **Success seems to come easy for them**. They keep growing and thriving despite the crises and chaos out in the world. How is it possible?

Here's the thing: these people do not have a "magic wand." They may have learnt how to leverage decisions and choices, with the potential to position themselves to have the best in whatever situation, overcome, and thrive. You too, can. YOU can get the same or even better results.

If you want success and thriving as a lifestyle, it is possible. One of the major ways would be for you to become an expert in your decision-making and your choices. **Would you like to know how this can happen?**

In this book, I have presented techniques that will enable you to develop perspectives for the exploration of effective decision-making processes, which in turn will enable you to effectively navigate various aspects of your life.

You will learn principles and you will be equipped with tools that will open your mind to new possibilities, and give you opportunities to create stability even in an unstable world. There's no more time for you to **stand in your own way.** Let's take this journey together, so you can have the life you deserve. You are made to succeed and to THRIVE. Take responsibility and be accountable.

Chapter One

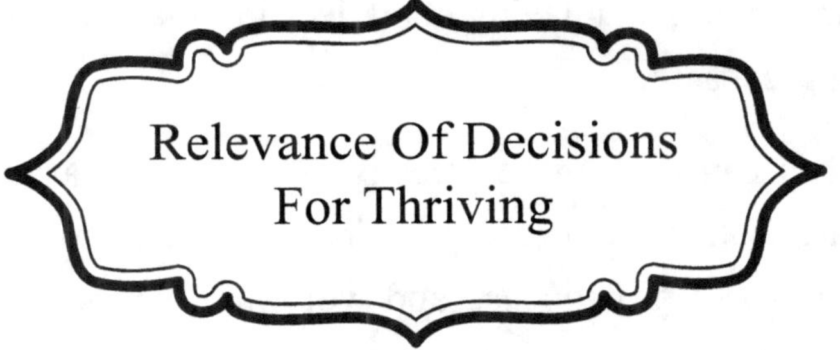

Change hits—sometimes suddenly and without warning. Things become disrupted. When this happens, what are the "must-take decisions," and which should pivot towards the "must-have outcomes" connected to the developments and your priorities?

In any situation, a skill and tool that is available to you to work towards a relatively stable environment is your ability to decide and your choices. Decisions are important, and having good decision-making ability is a great asset.

You can only make effective decisions in areas that are within your control. Focus on that. When the unexpected happens, and you find yourself going down into the valley, into the pit of despair, and you are aware of possible decisions that have brought you to that situation, review your options and recalibrate. Your next decisions could stop the descent and provide the stepping stones for your rebound and restoration to the path of your choice.

In any situation, it is up to you to make right choices

and decisions; what you need to continue doing, stop, or start doing. Poor choices and decisions are life impeders and destroyers.

Our world is shifting and changing at a fast rate. The comfort people were used to, has been challenged. Foundations shaken, shattered, and requiring repair. Previously secured and assured persons are losing relevance with their old craft and becoming panicky. What worked well for decades, has lost effectiveness, leaving safety and the future threatened as life looks tougher.

Pulling back the curtain, the premises on which decisions were made, have been radically altered, with current and emerging circumstances requiring different ways of coping with new realities. Delays in readjusting carry high risks and are costly.

To succeed and thrive therefore requires quick adaptation and a flexible mindset. In this time and age, there's hardly much that is cast in stones that survive for long. Effectively adjusting on the go has become the new mantra for an effective lifestyle, and coping with the "fluid world."

Decisions are vital, and responding appropriately in decision-making, is a critical factor for thriving in any season. Some decisions require a great deal of urgency. Others allow a more reasonable time frame to consider the available options for adoption. There is a place for proper consultation, as a part of making the right decisions. So, never assume you are alone; tap into all available resources to make decisions that are best suited to your situation. You can turn your awful situation into an eventual delight.

For your decisions to set you up to thrive sustainably, some fundamentals are necessary. Below are some building blocks as examples:

i. Being in touch with reality and with real-time knowledge, having awareness of critical developments in your environment and operating contexts, and how they impact you and your situation.

ii. Being clear on what your decision objectives are, and your success indicators.

iii. An assessment of your current, against your desired state, and establishing the gaps to close to attain and sustain success for you to thrive.

iv. Adoption of an effective decision-making process, delivering outcomes to close your identified gaps.

v. Being realistic, pragmatic and flexible in your adaptation to reflect and integrate relevant inputs from the ever-changing landscape into your configuration and important considerations.

vi. Carefully analysing the decision to make, and undertaking the process to deliver the most effective outcome(s) suitable for your specific situation(s).

vii. In the short, medium and long term, undertake a reiterative process of reviewing and updating your approach for appropriate and optimum outcomes of your decisions against the circumstances at any moment.

viii. Others

Putting your specific circumstances into consideration

and perspective, the bottom line is for you to be current and choose to make the decision that is sustainable—the one that serves you the most—in attaining your intended goal in the best possible and most effective way.

What is the most suitable and appropriate move for you in your situation?

What are you to move away from, and/or move towards, to appropriately meet your distinct and unique needs?

This is not necessarily about what works for everybody. There is thoroughness in sifting and integrating information and other inputs that are useful for your situation. When you base and craft your decisions on this consistent basis, you are building up a momentum that helps you live at your best, thrive and keep thriving. Overall, you live, reaping the good rewards of your well-thought-out decisions.

Opt for and embrace the disciplines of making effective decisions, instead of going with the quick fixes.

Chapter Two

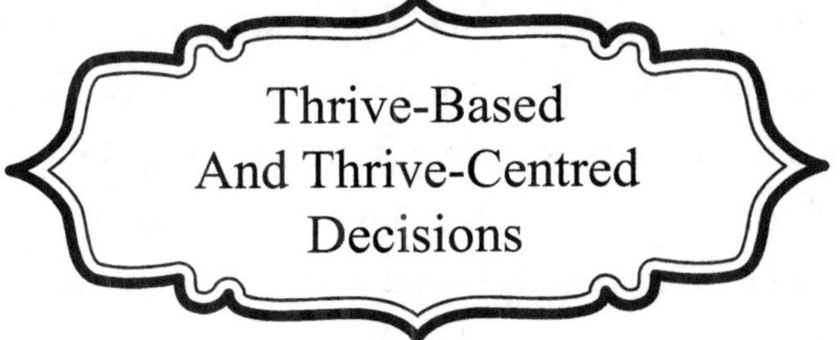

SOME POSSIBLE REASONS FOR INDECISIONS/INEFFECTIVE DECISIONS

The inability to make decisions or making ineffective decisions are major factors that hold people back from opportunities and great possibilities in life, career and business. It prevents them from attaining their full potential.

Possible factors that hinder people in respect of indecision and/or making ineffective decisions include fear of the unknown, 'scarcity mindset', people pressures, procrastination, self-doubt, lack of confidence or feelings of inadequacy, faulty perspectives or involvement in the blame game, not asking and answering the right questions, not consulting the right persons, not giving decision-making a priority because of 'time constraints' or not prioritising the decision(s) to be made, ignorance of the consequences of not making a decision or the right decision, amongst other limiting beliefs and actions.

A decision that is not aimed at delivering the best

outcome is a missed and wasted opportunity.

Thrive-Based And Thrive-Centred Decisions

I see thrive-based and thrive-centred decisions as decisions you arrive at, after going through an effective thorough process. In the end, you are satisfied that you took into consideration all relevant factors, and undertook proper efforts to make a decision that delivered the best outcomes you desired for your situation, and which set you up to thrive.

Life and living involve a series of decision points. We must think carefully and weigh the decisions we make to ascertain whether they are the decisions we want. Since our decisions make us, we should consider the overall situation and choose to capitalise on making the best decisions.

We are different, and there isn't a particular way for all to live life. There's also no specific approach to the issues that shows up every day. We approach life differently and have individual ways that best suit us to thrive. Your power, as well as your advantage, is that you are you. This is your leverage for contributions and to making a difference.

For you to thrive, how best you know yourself, and your ability to deploy and apply that knowledge, capitalising on your uniqueness, could be the factor that sets you apart and gives you an edge.

If you have read my previous book, ***Thriving On Who You Are,*** you probably recognise some of the familiar thoughts that I have represented here.

In this section, I want to apply my Signature **T. H. R. I. V. E** Model, as a framework applicable for decision making. The essence is to provide a structure that may be helpful for you to uniquely and effectively process your thoughts and ideas, in coming up with decisions that will set you up to thrive.

The following is the application of the Model, using the adapted case of Mombola, one of my coaching clients (his name has been changed to protect confidentiality).

THE T.H.R.I.V.E MODEL

T - The situation which you may currently be in, which needs intervention

H - Happenings and effects, impacts or manifestations of the situation

R - Root cause(s) identification for resolution

I - Ideal state, or the imagined outcome or end state you desire, and the gap identified and established against current reality

V - Verification and validation of the options available to you for adoption to move towards your goal(s)

E - Execute and embed your option(s) with specific action steps to move you to your desired end state, and thrive while tracking your progress.

APPLICATION OF THE MODEL TO MOMBOLA'S SITUATION

T - The situation he was in, which needed intervention

Mombola identified that what often trips him, and gets in his way of success and thriving, is his sudden burst of anger and uncontrolled reactions. His inability to effectively regulate and manage his emotions.

H - Happenings and effects, impacts or manifestations of the situation

This identified behaviour would leave him greatly ashamed, disappointed, miserable and confused after he has reacted explosively in situations, that he later regrets. Due to this known behaviour and approach, some of his peers deliberately press his vulnerable spot buttons, to trigger his anger. This occasionally takes him off track from what is most important at that moment. Mombola realised this situation has the potential to threaten and stall his career progression.

Within the company he works, some of the labels used to identify him because of his behaviour, include the following — abrupt, unregulated, impulsive, thoughtless, not in control, unguarded, unfiltered in speech, impetuous, quick to anger, and makes decisions in anger, can't rule his mind, dishonours others, not checking the stories he tells himself about others, etc. He didn't like it, so he decided **he is ready and willing to do the work for a change.**

Mombola decided to dig deeper to know himself better and tackle this challenge.

He got real with himself, invested and committed to doing the necessary work. Having realised his flaws, he desired a turnaround. He knew his turning point must begin with a personal decision for a change, followed by subsequent consistent right decisions and actions, to reinforce outcomes that would lead closer to his desired end state. He got ready and was intentional in attacking the root causes, and doing the work for his transformation. He wanted insights. He wanted to understand his behaviour. What makes him react the way he does? He wanted to look at and work on his thinking, assumptions, mental and emotional state and belief system. He wanted to know what his real standards are, generally. How does he see his world? The triggers that make him act the way he does, where do they come from? He wanted to reflect on everything to better understand himself and his current situation, as a launching pad for where he wants to go, and the outcomes he wants to achieve. He believed this process would help and empower him to self-explore and self-reflect, and enable him to make better choices and decisions for himself.

R - Root cause(s) identification for resolution

Mombola thought that his situation of constant agitation and lack of emotional control was biological. He grew up to know himself that way. He also knows a few other persons he believes are like him; they would erupt if circumstances that demanded such a response arose. Mombola said he was not amongst those with the gift of being "cool, calm and collected." Occasionally though, he admired them, and once in a while, wished to be like them.

Mombola also thought that it is difficult to trust people. According to him, "People you easily trust can easily disappoint you." Therefore, one of the ways he used to check if he could trust anyone, was to leverage on any of the labels used to identify him. If anyone could put up with Mombola long enough and still delivers on his expectations, then, he or she earns the status of being trustworthy.

Following the series of incidents, feedback and backlashes, Mombola first began to consult with himself. On his own, he probed and explored, wanting to find out the main source(s) of his behaviour. He talked with a few trusted advisors, including some of the persons he considered had the gift of being "cool, calm and collected." He also eventually decided to work with a professional coach.

Mombola was desirous to get to the root of the problem and identify his reactions or responses which he had begun to consider and see as undesirable in certain situations. Those would become areas of specific focus to move away from, and they would paint clear pictures of the new desired state to move towards in realising the **new vision of his future self.**

From the various sources Mombola employed to work on getting relevant inputs and support, the following lessons began to emerge for him:

i.   The capacity to be aware of, manage, and express one's emotions, and to handle interpersonal relationships judiciously and empathetically is not something inherited or strictly biological.

ii.   The situation we all experience are most often neutral. Whether or not we realise it, most of our emotions are products of our thinking concerning the situation we are going through. Our thoughts and inner "self-talk" about what's happening, lead to our decisions and how we behave.

iii.   His realisation to pay more attention to the thoughts that may be driving his emotions, was key to the road of his emotional regulation.

iv.   If he becomes aware of the thoughts that create his emotions, he then will have the power to readjust those thoughts, so that they engender a different approach to managing his situations and behaviour.

I - Ideal state, or the imagined outcome or end state he desired, and the gap identified and established against current reality

Mombola realised that what he needed was an inside-out change or transformation, thus, he established his WHY for embarking on his desired change process. They include the following:

i.   He wants to manage his relationships better and earn respect as a professional leader.

ii.   To become a better enabler contributing to enhancing teamwork and higher levels of productivity.

iii. He didn't want to settle for the short-term gain and the sense of being an "authoritative and no-nonsense leader," at the expense of the long-term gains and interests of being a respected leader, who is self-driven, able to mobilise his team to voluntarily produce the desired results.

iv.   He wants to live a more contented and fulfilled life.

v. Successful transformation for him can qualify him to be a change agent or leader, helping others with similar situations.

vi. Success will contribute to enhancing his career progression.

With the above personal discoveries, Mombola crafted the **VISION** of his ideal state, or the imagined outcome and end state as follows:

"I am designed to have emotions, and it is part of who I am. I confirm that my emotions are not bad. I am cultivated, respected and recognised to have trained and mastered my mind to be stronger than my emotions. I show up to present myself as I desire to be in any situation. I am not exhibiting the default mode which people seem to have pigeonholed me, or thoughtlessly yielding to my emotions at play at the moment, and as they come up."

"My relationships are well managed, and when I find myself going in the old route, I immediately catch myself and return to the new path of my dream and vision. I am a well-tempered **Business Leader.** I do not have to be anyone else. I am an evolved, better person and leader."

V - Verification and validation of the options available to him for adoption to move towards his goal(s)

Mombola continued to assess and check himself. He asked what was happening within him when he found himself behaving in the ways he wanted to move away from. He looked for what to eliminate and what was feeding his undesirable state. He identified what to move towards within the next 6 months to 1 year and began to pinpoint some of the specific issues to tackle and focus on. They included the following:

Move From	Move To
Abrupt	Measured response/More calculated/Cultivated
Unregulated	More regulated response
Impulse	Conditioned/Intentional/Deliberate
Thoughtless	Thoughtful
Feeling not in control	To be more in control
Unguarded (utterances)	Guarded
Unfiltered speech	Filtered
Impetuous	Thinking things through
Decision while angry	Decision while sober
Not ruling my mind	Training and mastering my mind to see the good and bad in every situation

Express feelings in a way that dishonours	Express feelings in a way that is honouring
Emotions ruling me	I regulate my emotions
Not being able to choose my response	I am able to choose my response
Quick to anger	Slow to anger
Constant anger	Momentary anger
My thoughts hold me in captivity	My thoughts are under control
Not checking the stories I tell myself	Checking and verifying the stories I tell myself
Presumptuous of people and situations	Taking each situation/person on the assessed merits

Change or Transformation Ideas and Strategies

Mombola began to see things differently. He learnt new principles of how working to change his situation, beginning with his **thoughts and beliefs,** are a critical part of his transformation journey. He understood why it was necessary to retrain his brain to create a mindset of success which he has now defined. He saw this will deliver the **LEADERSHIP STYLE** in the direction he desired to go. Additional emerging reinforcing lessons he got are:

i.   A leader's leadership style is related or connected to his personality, skill, knowledge, experience and context.

ii.   A good leader will be able to assess a given situation and adopt a style of leadership that will best achieve the results he is looking for.

iii.   Quite often, many leaders rely on their default personal style of leadership, only changing when forced to, through circumstance.

iv.   A leader needs to always check whether his style is the best for him in his situation. Does it bring out the best in the people and deliver the expected (best) results?

At this point, what he believed was changing. This began to influence what he did and how he related with people. He realised that what he sets his mind on, is what will trigger his thoughts and behaviours.

Mombola agreed to the specific activities with timelines to be undertaken, including those for reprogramming his mindset, in line with his change and transformation objectives. He identified tools, resources and accountability partners to support him in the process.

E - Execute and embed his option(s) with specific action steps to move him to his desired end state, and thrive while tracking his progress.

Wrapping up his work, Mombola categorised areas of focus for execution. He tracked his progress, embedded the lessons and transition ideas into his life and work style, into four groups as follows:

i.   To capitalise on areas where his current approach works in achieving his desired objectives — being authentic to himself.

ii.   To improve the identified areas of his lesser strengths and weaknesses that could easily trump him, if not intentionally handled.

iii.   Look at the areas of further opportunities still open to him to grow in his leadership influence and results, invest in them, and

iv.   To stick with the strategies or tools, resources and support aimed at minimising the impacts of areas that potentially open doors for him to fall back to where he had decided to move away from.

Mombola realised that for him to ultimately succeed, he needed focus, consistency, discipline and the identified support to sustain his newly gained momentum for moving towards his desired ideal state and destination. He was internally motivated, excited, willing and committed to doing just that.

Owning your approach

You can thrive based on well-considered decisions that fit and are in alignment with who you are, and possess benefits for others within your scope of influence. Opening up and working on changing limiting beliefs can change things for you.

i. What is your style and approach to decision-making?

ii. How do you develop a lifestyle of making thrive-based and thrive-centred decisions?

iii. What could your own personalised plan look like?

iv. What will you build into it to stay on course, and achieve your ultimate objective(s)?

There could be different processes, systems, approaches and models for everyone. We have however in this section used my Signature **T. H. R. I. V. E** Model, as a guide for making decisions that can set you up to thrive.

Deciding and Committing to the Process

Change may be difficult, but it's always better than remaining in an undesirable state and condition. This illustrated case with Mombola involves committing to realising a specific desired objective. Not all decisions require this kind of exhaustive process. You have to decide. The **T. H. R. I. V. E** or other Models may be relevant to some of your situations and can be leveraged holistically in a progressive way to areas you intend to make well-considered and thought-out decisions. Your endeavours must be accompanied by the willingness to do the work in developing a lifestyle of making thrive-based and thrive-centred decisions with the ultimate aim of delivering the best results for your situation.

Chapter Three

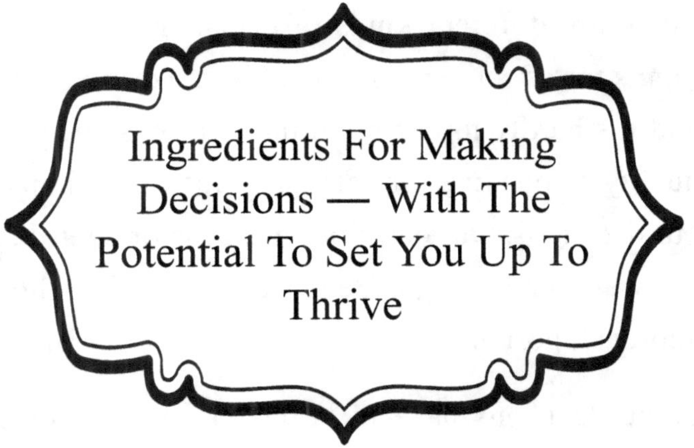

Ingredients For Making Decisions — With The Potential To Set You Up To Thrive

If you want your decisions to work for you, respect and apply the principles for effective decision-making. Decisions are cultivated for the desired outcomes. Do not expect to reap what you have not cultivated. You have to become intentional to win. You also have to be intentional in letting your quality decisions provide you with an edge in every situation of life.

There are different kinds of decisions, with different inputs for effectiveness. Sometimes, we are not aware, and it's hardly top of mind that our existence and the quality of our lives are at stake, due to the impacts of our decisions. Our decisions are a major contributor to the way our lives go. Being hasty and thoughtless in approach portends risks.

Some decisions have to be taken on the spur of the moment. Others allow time for consideration of available options. Having a system, and intentionally applying wisdom to guide your decision-making could improve the quality of the decisions, and be the difference maker, that contributes to setting you up to thrive.

Below are some suggested input ideas to factor into your approach for enhanced quality decision-making. These input ideas have the potential to get you to your desired ideal place and to thrive. They are:

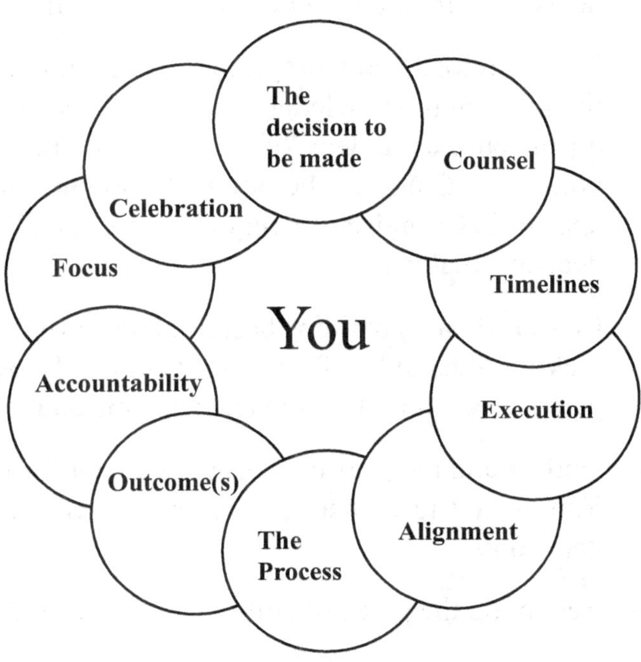

You as the decision maker:

i.   You are central to enabling the decision-making approach, and for it to work effectively.

ii.   Be honest with yourself. Focus on you, and what is within your control. Acknowledge where you are. Create and align decisions that will move you to what and the best you want to become.

iii. Make it top of mind that the outcomes of your decisions are intended to advance your life.

iv.   Feed, preload, and programme your mind with thoughts and knowledge on how to thrive, and on thriving as a way of life – 'your mind rules your life'. Come to the point of knowing that an appropriate mindset is a required base for effective decision-making.

v.   Live and learn. Avoiding haste and rush in decision-making—devoid of consideration of overall perspective, possible impacts and consequences.

vi.   Understand the priorities of the moment for focus. You cannot just trust your feelings to make good decisions.

vii. Reflect on the place of culture and relevant factors

for your context.

viii. Be aware of your limitations —not knowing all the facts and answers—and remain curious and open to asking relevant questions, to consider different perspectives and ideas that will stretch you beyond your comfort zone.

ix. Take responsibility for your decisions as a part of your personal journey. Lead and drive the process.

x. Recognise and reflect on your biases, and plan to mitigate and resolve their impacts without compromising your decisions.

xi. Probe, explore and dig deeper into your beliefs and values that are working in your favour, or getting in the way of your success.

xii. Recognise the place of your intuition, discernment or inner promptings, as well as unexpected "extraordinary downloads," as inputs for your decisions. Determine how you will handle them while remaining responsible and accountable for your decisions.

xiii. Be bold and courageous to take decisions that will serve you the most in the situation.

xiv. Take overall ownership of the decisions, and implement your actions.

The decision to be made:

i. Evaluate whether or not the situation actually requires a decision to be made. Establish your priorities.

ii. Establish your WHY for making the decision— your objective or rationale— and the actual problem you want to solve, or the vision you want to achieve.

iii. Properly identify and define the problem; leverage your focus on solving that specific problem.

iv. Keep abreast of macro developments in areas of your decision interests; identify and glean insights on what could be a relevant consideration for input.

v. Verify if the decision to be made is solely your responsibility.

vi. Be concerned with the short, medium and long-term impacts of the decision on you and others.

vii. Constantly update your decision in line with emerging realities.

Relevance of Counsel:

i. Be humble, know and learn where and when to seek good counsel and feedback, using trusted associates and experts as sounding boards.

ii. Often challenge your decision-making process or construct, and modify where and when necessary.

iii. Co-create with relevant partners, as may be necessary, adopting a process that creates the best outcomes.

Decision timelines:

i. Review the appropriateness of the timelines for making and implementing your decisions. Correct decisions become ineffective when made and/or implemented at the wrong time.

Execution of the decision:

i. Build an execution plan for your decision-making by breaking your execution steps into required phases and milestones.

ii. Weigh your capacity and capability, including your resources to execute and sustain the implementation of your decision.

Seeking Alignment:

i.   Consider what ongoing collaboration or support you might need at any stage of your process.

ii. Take as a priority, possible consequences for relevant stakeholders and how to manage them.

iii. Assess the general alignment of your decision with your specific and/or overall contexts.

The decision-making process:

i.   Adopt a sound and effective process and trust the process. Monitor, tweak and adapt as you go.

The outcomes of the decision:

i.   Your decisions impact others. Decide responsibly. Where possible, avoid or mitigate adverse consequences.

ii. Be open and flexible. Learn how to handle and manage unexpected outcomes, including quicker or delayed results.

iii. Catch yourself, and self-correct when you are running away from realities that demand you to change. Stretch into who you have not been before, and undertake what you have not done before.

Accountability Partners:

i. As necessary, identify accountability partners to keep you on track with what you have decided, and to support you in getting the intended results.

Keeping focus:

i. Watch your implementation steps, keep away from distractions, and focus on turning the decision into reality.

ii. Patiently work and wait for the results.

iii. Lean into your faith, and hope for the best outcome(s).

Celebration:

i. Have fun; celebrate achieving your milestones.

Incorporating the above ideas into your decision-making can be likened to an artist with a brush and a canvas. He carefully chooses and selects the colours and strokes; being intentional in magnifying what stands out, to put out the best artwork with the most desired powerful impact. Every bit of the process is a creative and decision point.

Decisions set you up to thrive. Become skilful in what you choose as input factors to your decision-making process. Identify and focus on articulating and integrating only elements that will enable you to produce suitable and sustainable masterpiece decisions for your situations.

Integrating an effective process into your decision-making has the potential to boost your ability to thrive. The choices and combination of factors as inputs for the same decision could be different for everyone. When you choose the right decision for your situation, it will keep you on track in getting to your specific intended destination.

Earn a reputation and recognition for carefully making decisions that set you up to thrive. Connect more to thrive-based and thrive-centred decision-making approaches. Sow decision seeds embedded with success and thrive DNA for your situations and life.

In putting the relevant elements together, and operationalising these for decision-making—and as

an antidote to making rash decisions—below may be **an optional guide** and possible alternative to the **T. H. R. I. V. E** and other models:

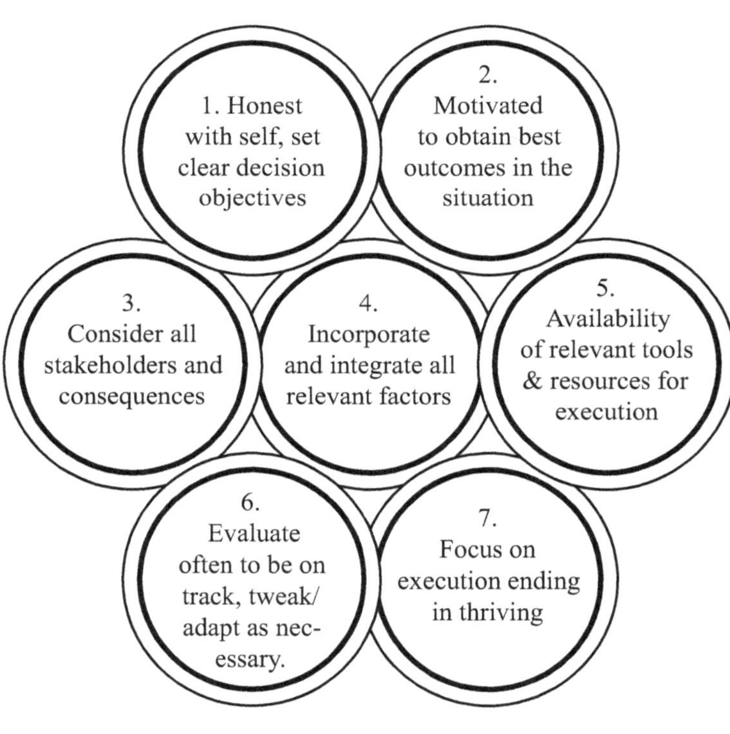

1. Honest with self, set clear decision objectives
2. Motivated to obtain best outcomes in the situation
3. Consider all stakeholders and consequences
4. Incorporate and integrate all relevant factors
5. Availability of relevant tools & resources for execution
6. Evaluate often to be on track, tweak/adapt as necessary.
7. Focus on execution ending in thriving

Chapter Four

MY PERSONAL CASE STUDY & LESSONS ON THRIVING

From experience, I have learnt that despite considering all relevant factors during decision-making, unexpected and unintended consequences still happens. Decision(s) may not be as infallible as we want them to be.

Let me share a personal story:

I Needed A Job Change

The company I was working with was experiencing serious financial challenges which impacted the regular frequency of payment of monthly salaries. There were months in which monthly salaries were paid well into the new month. I wasn't the only one affected by the company's financial challenges. My family was affected. The situation was that I met my wife at this job, we got married, had our two children and continued to work there.

To cushion the impact of late payment of monthly

salaries, I decided to use my personal vehicle to transport passengers. I would wake up early at 5:00 AM, and go out to transport passengers to have sufficient funds to cater for food for the day. By 7:00 AM, I would be back home to prepare for work and by 8:00 AM, I would be at the office.

Fortunately, we lived in the company quarters close to the manufacturing plant where my office was located. My decision to transport passengers, though not palatable and pleasant, was what gave us extra income, and I continued to do this for a while. My wife was sad over my decision and our situation, where I had to stress myself the way I did to provide for the family.

After a while, my colleague saw a job advert she believed I was suited for and told me about it. The issue was that the job was in Lagos while my wife and I were working and living outside of Lagos. When my colleague mentioned the name of the company advertising the job, it was unfamiliar, so I was not interested. I decided not to apply for the job. The two weeks period indicated for the applications of interested candidates ran out and expired.

Soon after, I was in a meeting when it was mentioned to us at the end, that there were "rumours" going around that the price of petrol will be increased by the government the following day. I became quite concerned. I knew that when fuel prices increase, the general cost of living goes up. That would compound and complicate the already "bad" situation I was going through with my family.

The thoughts of that job advert, which candidates' application timeframe had expired began to fill my mind. The news of a possible fuel price increase became a trigger for me and I saw this as my second chance. Even though the door had been shut, in terms of when interested candidates could apply, I believed I could knock on it. Quickly, I reviewed and revisited my earlier decision not to apply for the role. I got relevant stakeholders onboard and aligned within my family, in respect of the latest developments and we agreed that I should send in my application for the role, against my earlier decision. Not only did I knock on that door that had been shut, but it was also opened to admit me in. Yes. I got the job without even knowing anyone in that company.

With hindsight, I saw that my human limitations set in to initially hinder me from applying for that job. To us, some things are plain and somewhat obvious. Others are not. The question then is, when things are not plain and obvious about the decision to make, what can you do to make an appropriate decision?

In my situation, I saw that providence was on my side. I got that job that changed my situation and that of my family. That job and the company became the opportunity that opened the door for me to work, not only in my home country, Nigeria, but also as an expatriate in four other countries outside of Nigeria.

Here are some of the lessons I learnt from that situation:

i. You are responsible for doing everything to make decisions, incorporating all inputs and factors that will enable you to have the best outcomes in every decision-making situation.

ii.   In many instances, decisions you have made, may not be "cast in stones" and permanent. Decisions may not be foolproof.

iii. Take one step at a time, and incorporate what you know at the moment for decision-making while remaining realistic and humble to revisit your decisions, if it becomes necessary.

iv.   Be open and sensitive to developments with and around you. Learn what possible tweaks and changes to make to decisions you may have made, incorporating the most recent events and developments. As earlier mentioned in Chapter 3, also recognise the place of your intuition, discernment or inner promptings, unexpected "extraordinary downloads" as inputs for your decisions, while you remain responsible and accountable for the decisions.

v.   Some decisions will remain in the work-in-progress category, and not final.

vi.   You can often start again when it becomes necessary.

vii. Remember you are human and not all-knowing. There are lots of factors outside your control.

viii. Flexibility and agility could help you recover lost ground, as a result of previous wrong decisions, or decisions that aren't working out the way you intended. Taking a corrective decision can help you rebound to achieve your ultimate goals.

ix. Your decisions make you. The decisions you make must be weighed carefully and seriously at all times, and with all the importance they deserve.

Everybody's experience will be different. The moral of my story is for you to always want the best for yourself when you're in any situation that requires you to make decisions. Adjust or adapt as may be appropriate, to come up with decisions that will set you up to thrive. This will depend on what you see evolving in the events after you have taken some of your decisions. For instance, the personal stories you may want to create and tell out of those events, the voice you want to give to the events and how that can help you become better as well as achieve your vision of a better you.

Revisiting and reviewing your earlier decision, like in my case, may be your second or another chance to launch into your open possibilities and opportunities, as well as positively impacting others in your world.

Corrective decisions may often be required when previous decisions do not work out as intended. In going through this process to review and revisit the decisions you had earlier made, the ideas highlighted about making effective decisions in this book, remain available for you as a guard, check posts and as supporting tools for your inputs and careful considerations.

Be aware of the conversations going on within you. Be willing to change course when changing course is considered the best option and move. Adopting the mindset of what it means to *thrive* as defined in this book, can be the recipe that helps to sustain your advancement, setting you up for success.

Thriving is moving towards your goals and vision, in the midst of and despite your challenging situations and events. In the process, you keep adapting, adjusting, evolving, and coming out better equipped to live life, leveraging on your newly acquired experience and competencies in helping others become better.

Chapter Five

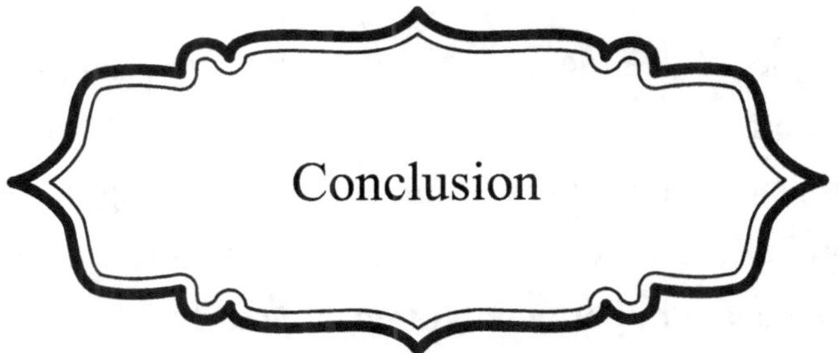

Conclusion

Many times when we look at ourselves, we do not see what and who we can become. One of the ways by which we develop and become who we eventually will be is by making effective decisions that build on one another.

You can envision the kind of future you want and align your decisions to realise that vision. Your decisions play a vital role in determining the way your life goes.

Some of the decisions you make are complex and require lots of input factors, analysis and deep considerations. Others are simple, requiring little input and effort. However, all decisions and the choices you make, are important and impact your life.

i.   What decisions do you make daily?

ii. Are they bringing you to realise your visions and dreams or not?

It's crucial to decide carefully with the consequences in mind.

Make your well-considered moves. Set yourself up to

win, succeed and thrive with your decisions. Believe that your decisions are fundamental in determining the direction your life goes, and let this conviction be foundational. It is your right belief that motivates your right actions.

Become an expert in making thrive-based and thrive-centred decisions. Embody thrive-centredness as a way of life. Be open and flexible to readily adjust in your decision-making, incorporating relevant inputs that serve and support you well. As highlighted in this book, a rigid mindset could stand in your way.

Constantly update your decisions in line with current realities. Your circumstances and situations can change. You have the power with your decisions to stay in control of how things turn around. Challenge yourself to press in and stay engaged in the process of shaping the way your life goes, with intentional decisions, leveraged at taking you to your preferred destination.

When you see ahead of you what you want and believe is possible, and become set to achieve it, you kick start your vision realisation journey. Clarify exactly what you need to move forward and towards it. Wait no more. Decide and take action.

Giving up on yourself, to go back to living a life you know is beneath what you are made for should not be an option. Keep leveraging on your resourcefulness, and the options available to you.

With your decisions and choices, launch yourself into your desired future. Your intended cherished future, will not just happen. Even in troubled and uncertain times, you can set yourself up to thrive with your decisions entrenching you in creating exceptional value for our world. Decide and execute your actions to realise your visions.

Get into the consistent process of thoroughly weighing and considering your important decisions, in such a way as to help move your life to your best-desired outcomes. Progressively transform who you are by making and effectively executing your decisions. Practice this as a way of life, and as a way of setting yourself up to thrive.

ABOUT THE AUTHOR

Samson Umurhurhu is the CEO of **Thrive Coaching Centre and HR Consulting Services Limited,** a company that focuses on Leadership/Executives, Talents/Strengths, Team/ Group Coaching, as well as installing a Coaching Culture in Organisations.

He is also the Chief Business Facilitator of **The Thrive Place Limited,** a one-stop hospitality facility in Lagos, Nigeria.

Samson also works with people to facilitate a smooth transition from paid employment to self-work and entrepreneurship.

He consults on Human Resources Strategies, especially in the areas of leadership development, employee engagement, and mobilization to realise set goals.

He holds a bachelor's degree in Sociology as well as a master's degree in Industrial and Labour Relations. He is a Certified Professional Coach and a Certified Master Coach with the Center for Coaching Certification, USA. He is certified as a Strengths Coach by the Gallup Organization and credentialed by the International Coaching Federation as a Professional Certified Coach (PCC).

Samson has extensive work experience in various core areas of the Human Resources Function from the Country, Regional, and Zonal levels, up to the Group Head Office of the Nestle Group, and effectively supported top-level management committees.

He is passionate about partnering with his clients in a way that frees them up to thrive against their odds, drives results to boost their levels of success and achieves desired objectives.

Samson lives in Lagos, Nigeria with his family. *Setting Yourself Up To Thrive With Decisions,* is his fourth book, after *Thriving Against The Odds – 15 Ideas*

For Professionals, Executives & Leaders To Sustain Advancement (2018), Who Wants A Coach (2020), and Thriving On Who You Are (2022)

www.thrivecoachandhr.com
Phone numbers: +234(0) 7081369471;
+234(0) 9063608987
E-Mail: info@thrivecoachandhr.com